Cowboys at Heart

Glenn Dromgoole

SOURCEBOOKS, INC.
NAPERVILLE, ILLINOIS

Published by Sourcebooks, Inc.
P.O. Box 4410, Naperville, Illinois 60567-4410
(630) 961-3900
FAX: (630) 961-2168
www.sourcebooks.com

ISBN-13: 978-1-4022-0567-5
ISBN-10: 1-4022-0567-8

Printed and bound in China
LEO 10 9 8 7 6 5 4 3 2 1

Introduction

The word "cowboy" came into the language after the Civil War, as cowboys—mostly young men, even boys—made the great cattle drives in the mid to late 1800s.

By the early 1900s, the mythological cowboy became the star of the silent movie, followed by the singing cowboy and the strong, courageous, independent, gun-slinging cowboy.

The cowboy emerged as the quintessential international hero, and a cowboy hat and pair of boots still remind us of a time when good guys wore white hats and bad guys wore black hats.

These days it's not always that easy to tell. But even today, cowboys—working ranch hands, rodeo daredevils, or cowboy painters, composers, writers—have important things to teach us about life, if we are open to their lessons.

Cowboys know who they are, wherever they are. The cowboy spirit can be embraced and embodied on the ranch or in the city, dressed in faded jeans or a business suit, driving a battered pickup or a new sedan. The true cowboy spirit is found on the inside, deep in the heart, in the substance of the soul.

Cowboys watch and listen.

A cowboy will tell you that a good rule for learning is to keep your eyes open and your mouth shut.

When cowboys get bucked off, they get back on.

And so must we. When we flunk a test, fail in a relationship, lose a big sale, or make a mistake that costs our team or company dearly, like the cowboy, we have to get back in there and try again.

Cowboys hang on when the going is tough.

A cowboy has to stay on a bucking bronc for eight seconds, which can seem like an eternity when you're the one riding. A good rule for us when facing tough times: try to hang on a little longer.

Cowboys respect each other.

They respect those who don't whine about their circumstances but just pitch in and do their job without a lot of fuss.

Cowboys are independent.

The cowboy is admired as tough, resilient, strong, courageous, and independent—values that are too often in short supply in today's world.

Cowboys
mend fences.

A good principle for everyone. Mend fences at home, at work, in all the arenas of our lives.

Cowboys have a good time.

Of course, it's not all work being a cowboy. When cowboys have a chance to unwind, they've been known to put a lot of gusto into their free time. They celebrate life. They enjoy living.

Cowboys get the job done.

Being a real cowboy—as opposed to those who just want to dress the part—is hard work. They don't expect things to come easy. They stay with it until the job is done.

Cowboys get the gate.

I f two cowboys riding in a pickup come to a closed gate, the one not driving is usually the one designated to get the gate—or open it. As with cowboys, the gates—the opportunities we come to—aren't going to open themselves.

Cowboys are often imitated.

If imitation is the sincerest form of flattery, then real working cowboys should feel honored. Most people who wear a cowboy hat or put on a pair of boots never have branded a calf or probably even ridden a horse, much less broken one. It takes a lot more than clothes to make a man, especially this type of man.

Cowboys are individuals.

Cowboys may share certain characteristics as a group, but no two cowboys are exactly alike. They don't all think alike. They don't all adhere to the same set of values. They don't all enjoy the same diversions. A cowboy is a person, with individual needs, opinions, beliefs, talents, and traits. Every cowboy is different—as we all are.

Cowboys know that life isn't always exciting.

The cowboy's job can often be as boring as anyone else's. Life doesn't always have to be exciting. We need those routine days to help us get our bearings, set our directions, and prepare us for the times when all hell breaks loose.

Cowboys understand quality.

A cowboy will invest wisely in a good pair of boots because he knows the investment will pay off in comfort and durability. Cutting corners may save a little money in the short run, but in the long run quality pays dividends.

Cowboys watch the sun rise.

A sunrise on the range—or anywhere else—calls our attention to the new day that lies before us—a day full of opportunities as well as challenges, surprises as well as routine tasks.

Cowboys respect animals.

To cowboys, a horse is respected as a partner, a dog as a friend, a bull as a worthy adversary. Cattle provide their livelihood and their very reason for being. If there weren't any cows, there wouldn't be any need for cowboys.

Cowboys need time alone.

We all need a little time alone with our thoughts, our dreams, our priorities, our values.

Cowboys like to tell stories.

The oral tradition is alive and well in the cowboy culture. Cowboys make time to listen to each other's stories, and especially to the stories of their elders. Stories entertain, enrich, inform, define, and connect us—as people with a past, a present, and a future.

Cowboys dress appropriately.

The cowboy style of dress is inherently casual, designed for cause and comfort. Cowboys can dress up when they have to, but they usually don't have to—or want to.

Cowboys savor wide open spaces.

Many of us long for the wide open spaces, where a person can get on his horse or in his pickup and ride for hours without seeing another soul; where we can watch the sun rise on a cool, clear morning and marvel at a glorious sunset in the evening and actually see the stars in all their majesty. Most of us have traded the wide open spaces for other perceived advantages of urban living. Cowboys haven't.

Cowboys like to cook—and eat.

The chuck wagon cook was an essential member of the trail drive team, and his reputation and influence continue with cook-offs, cookbooks, and restaurants that are as popular in cities as they are on the range. Cowboy cooking is intended for those with hearty—and appreciative—appetites.

Cowboys pick each other up.

In rodeos, the pick-up men have an important role to play. They are there to pick up the bronc-rider or bull-rider, whether he has successfully completed the ride or has been bucked off. We all need those in our lives who will pick us up when we're down and cheer for us when we're up.

Cowboys clown around.

Rodeo clowns have a serious purpose in their fun. They are there to protect cowboys from angry bulls. Humor often works that way for the rest of us as well.

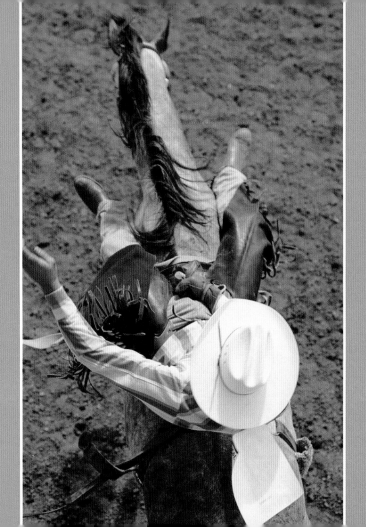

Cowboys are comfortable in the saddle.

The saddle is the cowboy's office. He may not be comfortable in all social situations, but in the saddle he is at home and confident. All of us have our comfort zones, where we are at our best. We should be careful in judging people's competence outside of their preferred environment.

Cowboys
are natural.

Cowboys don't offer a lot of pretense. They are who they are, and you can either accept them or not. A cowboy's word is his bond, as it should be with each of us.

Cowboys
understand.

Cowboys acquire what is called "cow
sense" or "horse sense." That is, they
learn to think like their customers (cattle)
and their partners (horses). They also
know what their bosses expect from them.
Whatever business or endeavor we're in,
we will be more successful if we can
understand the points of view and
expectations of our customers, our fellow
workers, and our bosses.

Cowboys sit on the fence for a reason.

It's the best seat in the house, it's available, and it's free. It's not because cowboys are indecisive or waiting to see which direction public opinion will take.

Cowboys enjoy a good song.

The singing cowboy is not completely a figment of Hollywood hype. On trail drives, cowboys would sing to keep the cattle from getting restless. Cowboys today may not sit around the campfire singing ballads, but they still appreciate a good cowboy song and admire cowboy singers. Cowboys or not, we ought to sing more— not to keep the cattle calm, but to soothe our own souls.

Cowboys wear different hats.

A cowboy might have a favorite work hat and another hat for going out on the town. A felt hat for fall, a straw hat for summer. Some cowboys even prefer caps, which don't cost nearly as much as custom hats. We all wear different hats in our various roles in life—parent, spouse, teacher, friend, voter, customer, worker. We are not just one personality wearing the same hat all the time but complicated individuals who cannot be easily labeled.

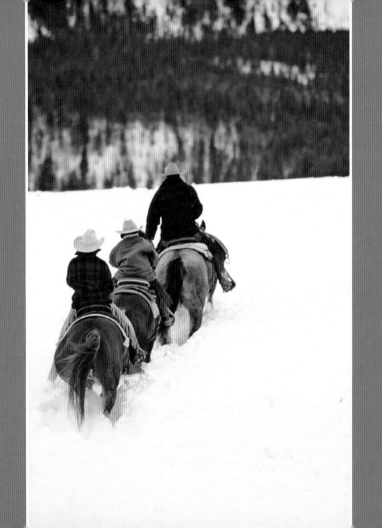

Cowboys see their job as a way of life.

I t's more than a living, being a cowboy. It's a way of life. And that way of life is what keeps cowboys doing what they do in spite of low pay, long hours, occupational dangers, and unforgiving climates.

Cowboys understand the need for heroes.

The cowboy movie stars of the old "B" westerns were mythical cowboys. They wore white hats and fancy clothes that never got soiled, and they rode into town just in time to save the day. The reel cowboys weren't real cowboys, but they gave several generations of youngsters someone to look up to. They made the cowboy an international icon that stood for positive values, courage, and right versus wrong.

Cowboys aren't afraid to get dirty.

Cowboying is a dusty, dirty job. But hard work that gets us dirty also sometimes can clear our minds and cleanse our souls. We need to get our hands dirty from time to time. We can always wash up.

Cowboys respect their heritage.

Cowboys have a rich heritage, beginning with the rough-and-tumble cattle drive days of the 1860s, '70s, and '80s. Our own heritage may not be as flamboyant and colorful as the cowboy's, but if we dig deep enough into our family history, we will find stories to tell, surprises to share, heroes to emulate, cowards to shun.

Cowboys believe in family values.

Cowboy families work together as families. They are more dependent on each other because they are more isolated than city families are. Everyone has chores to do. They pass along their beliefs in hard work, independence, contentment, determination, and self-worth. They take pride in who they are.

Cowboys see the big picture.

The view from a bluff, a cliff, or a mesa reminds us of the vastness, richness, and wonder of the world around us. It also puts our petty worries, grievances, jealousies, and pretensions into perspective.

Cowboys have an eye for beauty.

Especially when beauty clads itself in tight jeans.

Cowboys appreciate the sunset.

Sunset on the plains offers a spectacular array of colors signaling the winding down of a workday. It also suggests a moment to reflect on the pluses and minuses of the day: feeling a sense of gratitude in whatever accomplishments have come our way, learning from the failures we may have encountered, and perhaps finding a little humility in the fact that no one is perfect.

Cowboys like being together.

Cowboying is often a lonely life, so cowboys relish having an opportunity to be together. In our busy lives, most of us are around so many people that we tend to savor those opportunities to be alone. We need both.

Cowboys tip their hat.

A well-mannered cowboy invariably tips or removes his hat when he meets a woman. It's a polite gesture, a reflection of courtesy and respect. Good manners are a sign of strength, not weakness.

Cowboys make do.

Cowboys don't have to have all the latest high-tech equipment to do their job. A cowboy learns how to improvise, using a piece of baling wire or rope to fix nearly anything.

Cowboys understand the importance of teamwork.

We can't—and don't have to—do it all by ourselves. Like the cowboy, we need to form partnerships.

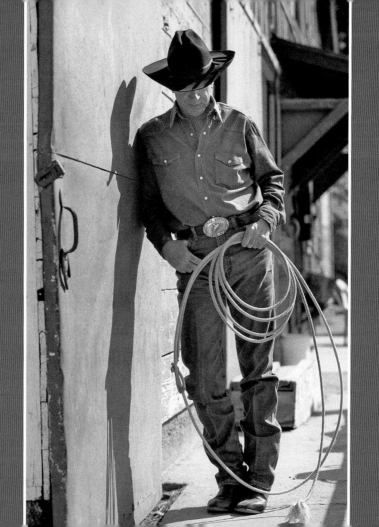

Cowboys have style.

Cowboy decor has spread from the ranch to the suburbs, from the bunkhouse to the bedroom, from the barn to the office. Cowboy style reminds us of simpler times and enduring values.

Cowboys know the territory.

Working cowboys know the terrain, the geography, the peaks and valleys of their ranch. Whatever our line of work, it is essential that we get to know the territory—not just the physical territory but the people, the language, the equipment, the inner workings of the job.

Cowboys
are reverent.

When you are as close to nature as cowboys are, you develop an inherent reverence for the spiritual side of life.

Cowboys enjoy the ride.

And so should we all.

Suggested reading

John Erickson's new edition of *The Modern Cowboy* offers an excellent description of what a cowboy's life is like today (University of North Texas Press, 2004).

More than twenty years ago, Douglas Kent Hall did a great job of capturing in interviews and pictures the story of *Working Cowboys* (Holt Rinehart & Winston, 1984).

Cowboy history and culture are related in art and text in *The Texas Cowboy*, with paintings and sculptures from the Texas Cowboy Artist Association, informative text by Donald Worcester, and an insightful introduction by Elmer Kelton (Texas A&M University Press, 1986).

Elmer Kelton has spent his life writing about cowboys. Two of his best novels concern the twentieth century cowboy—*The Good Old Boys* and *The Time It Never Rained* (available from St. Martin's Press and TCU Press). Also, see his essay on "Myth vs. Reality" in *My Kind of Heroes* (State House Press, 2004).

The Cowboy Way, edited by Paul Carlson, is a good collection of essays on a variety of topics related to cowboy history and culture (Texas Tech University Press, 2000).

Horsing Around, edited by Lawrence Clayton, Kenneth Davis, and Mary Evelyn Collins, offers a collection of essays, poems, and stories depicting contemporary cowboy humor (Texas Tech University Press, 1999).

Red Steagall discusses the cowboy way of life with more than twenty old-time cowboys and western actors and singers in *Cowboy Corner Conversations* (State House Press, 2004).

Three very good works on cowboy boots are *The Cowboy Boot Book* by Tyler Beard and Jim Arndt (Gibbs Smith, 1992) and their follow-up books—*Art of the Boot* (Gibbs Smith, 1999) and *Cowboy Boots* (Gibbs Smith, 2004).

Texas Bix Bender has written several humorous books on cowboy life and philosophy, including the instructive *Cowboy Etiquette* (Gibbs Smith, 2003).

Holly George-Warren teamed up with *Reader's Digest* to produce an informative and attractive book on the advent and influence of western movies, *Cowboy: How Hollywood Invented the Wild West* (Ivy Press, 2002).

About the Author

Glenn Dromgoole is the bestselling author of more than a dozen books, including *I'd Rather Be Fishing* and *What Happy Dogs Know*. He is managing editor of State House Press and McWhiney Foundation Press, publishing books on Texas and Civil War history.

Photo Credits